Cancer Can't Destroy Love

Learning to Cope

Barbara Creasy

Copyright ©2008
SonGlow Press, Nashville, Tennessee
All Rights Reserved

ISBN 978-0-6152-4209-5

A portion of the proceeds from this book will be donated to
the American Cancer Society "Relay for Life."

*This book is lovingly dedicated
to two very special people,*

*In Memory of
my father, Malcolm Denton Moore,
who left us way too suddenly
following his battle
with Pancreatic Cancer*

and

*In Honor Of
Katherine Kilcullen-Bergeron,
a dear friend,
currently waging war
with Uterine Cancer.*

Is this book for you?

Cancer can be devastating, not only to the person that has the disease, but also for family members and friends. In this book, you will find tools and support to help you in this battle, tools that will enrich your daily life and help you cope with grace.

You do not have to fight alone.

Written for the patient, caregiver, or friend, this book has one purpose, to encourage and remind you that you CAN overcome your discouragement whether you have cancer or not. Hope is a powerful weapon but once it is lost, life can be overwhelming. Here are the tools you will need.

Contents

Chapter	Page
Introduction	i
Chapter One The "Big C"	1
Chapter Two Getting Support	3
Chapter Three Sometimes You Cry	11
Chapter Four Healing	21
Chapter Five Creating Your Perfect Atmosphere	25
Chapter Six When Dark Days Come	37

Chapter Seven   45
    The Power of Positive Thinking

Chapter Eight   53
    Profiles in Courage

Chapter Nine   61
    After Cancer

Chapter Ten   65
    Fighting Back: The Relay for Life

Chapter Eleven   69
    Reflections on the Night:
    From the Survivor's Lap to the Luminaria

Chapter Twelve   77
    Resources
    Canada   78
    United States   83

Author's Note   88

Introduction

Bless you. I do not know what you are dealing with now or what you have gone through in the past, but you have picked up this book so that says a lot. As cancer eats away at the body, it wears you down, affects friends and family members, and may try to rob you of your good spirits as well. Tell cancer to take a hike. You are about to overcome the disease from deep inside yourself. It may think it won, but only physically.

This book has one purpose, to encourage and remind you that you CAN overcome your discouragement. Hope is a powerful weapon but once it is lost, life can be overwhelming.

You are not alone, even on the darkest days when it is easier to admit defeat than fight for one more minute. Yes, I understand, because I have been in your shoes and know how you feel. The one good thing about coping with adversity is that eventually, you pick up a few tricks along the way.

Some of the lessons I learned were hard ones, but share them with you now. For years, as I coped with a chronic illness, I ignored friends that told me to write a book about how I cope with life and remain upbeat most of the time. They felt it would inspire and encourage others. Although I learned many lessons worth sharing, I did not do so.

Then in the spring of 2007, as I wrote in my journal after the first Relay for Life after my father's death from cancer, the thoughts poured out, tumbling onto the page, until I realized that they required sharing with others. While originally for my eyes only, I knew that this book needed to be written. Others at different stages of this journey required help coping. They needed to know that they are not alone and could carry on.

Personally, I have not had cancer. However, before you discount what I have to share, know that not only have I been touched by cancer of loved ones and know your pain as a caregiver, I have had my own share of adversity. The tools and strategies that I learned as I dealt with a chronic illness and other hardships, have given me a wealth of knowledge that I share with you now. These experiences have made me stronger and have taught me how to cope with life.

The poem, "Feelings," on the next page, expresses not only the thoughts of cancer patients and their caregivers, but also those living with a chronic illness. Perhaps you will relate as well.

Be strong. Hang on. Lean on others when you need to but support others when you are able. My wish for you is that you are able to have peace in your heart as often as possible, and acceptance, when it is not.

Feelings

Sometimes you rejoice.
You wait … you are afraid.
You watch and study,
You hurt… you worry,
You need a hug.

Sometimes you are tired.
Tired of being sick,
Of being strong … and brave,
Of hiding your feelings,
Tired of being tired.

Sometimes, as a caregiver,
You are cheerful… cranky…
Scared… in control
You wish someone
would take care of you.

Sometimes you rejoice.
Other times you weep.
You try to forget.
You choose to remember.

~ Barbara Creasy

Chapter 1

The "Big C"

"You have Cancer."

When the doctor gives a cancer diagnosis, it is not like saying, "You have appendicitis." You can try leaving it alone, treating it, or it may require surgery. There is no easy answer.

No, a cancer diagnosis is different. It has a unique set of baggage other diseases do not have. Cancer is common enough that everyone knows about it, and most have been touched in some way.

There are survivors and you hope to be on that list. However, it is a long, hard road; a road that you did not choose. Cancer may affect you, a family member, or a co-worker. It is random and unfair.

Not everyone survives cancer, and even those that survive will face an uphill battle. No matter your chances, that knowledge fills your head day and night without your permission. Sure, there are treatments they can try. I say try, because they do not always work. The problem with cancer treatment is that sometimes, it seems worse than the disease itself.

The battle with cancer is a long, hard, slow process, full of emotional ups and downs, frustrations, celebrations, fears, and waiting. At times, there is overwhelming exhaustion, both mental and physical.

Cancer sometimes brings moments of hope and celebration. The test looked good. They did not find any more. It did not spread.

Finally, the words you dream of, "You beat it." First anniversary, fifth, tenth. Each milestone takes you away, though it is never totally gone from your head.

Cancer touches you permanently, sometimes physically, but always emotionally. Of course, you certainly can survive this disease, and many do survive, never affected by cancer again, but you do not survive untouched.

Chapter 2

Getting Support

No matter what you do in life, choosing a new chair, giving a report in history class, going on a diet, or walking home from school for the first time, it helps to have someone there to support you. It is even more important that someone be available when you deal with serious issues.

When you do the "big" things such as surgeries or meetings to discuss a treatment plan, people remember that you need support and are usually there for you. However, the daily life situations are the ones that get you down.

As a patient, you may have frustrations and fears that you do not want to share with family members. This may be because you do not want to worry them, you do not want to appear weak, or perhaps they are just tired of hearing about it! It does not mean that they do not care, but it is not the same for them. They feel helpless to meet your needs or solve your complaints.

You need someone that has dealt with what you are going through or is currently dealing with it, someone that truly understands how you feel. Support groups can provide a safe place to vent your frustrations and fears, ask questions, share solutions, and allow you to support others.

Caregivers also need to seek support from others. Sharing how tired you are does not mean that you love the person any less, but that you are just that, tired. Other caregivers understand that you may not want to complain to the patient. After all, he did not ask for that disease or condition! They realize that you are worried about the physical problems as well as the financial impact. Above all, other caregivers know that you feel overwhelmed. They can share solutions and give you hope.

Chapter Two   Getting Support

Having a support group gives you a safe place to share, a built-in group of caring individuals that are not personally involved. As you get to know people in your group, you may develop close friendships. The bond created because of illness may grow into a lifelong connection that spans many other areas beyond medical concerns. These groups are helpful for a wide variety of reasons.

Kath and I met each other almost fifteen years ago as members of an online support group for people with lupus. In the winter of 2006, she was diagnosed with cancer. Here is one of her updates sent in e-mail:

And the CT scan showed that the cancer has spread to my aortic lymph nodes and two places in my lungs..........

Today really sucked badly... and I am going to just crawl under the blankets and wish it all away....

Love & *Light*
Kath

Cancer Can't Destroy Love

There is little to add to these words. Some days are bad. There is no way around that, but sharing with others helps. Many had family members with cancer and we tried to help her by being there to listen.

We have shared our lives. While originally a group organized around a common disease, lupus, we bonded and became sisters as we fought our troubles together. Kath fought a long, hard battle with lupus and overcame so much.

When she was diagnosed with cancer, it shook us all to the core. After fighting so hard to accomplish the things that she had already won, it just seemed impossible for her to have yet another struggle to face, a war we did not know how to fight. We were devastated, but could only wait and pray with her.

Yet, there was a sense that somehow, Kath would not allow this to defeat her.

Our online support group had long provided a safe place at times so that we could vent, share,

Chapter Two Getting Support

and know others understood and cared when we could not share with family. We felt helpless, knowing all we could do was to "be there" in spirit, listening and waiting.

As much as others care and want to help, only someone going through the same thing truly understands. While your loved one is "there" for you, having additional support lightens the burden.

A support group provides an instant bond, people that can say, "I understand what you mean" and you know that they do because they either are facing it now or have in the past.

Just having something in common does not mean that it is the group for you. Once I attended a meeting of people with a similar condition. After an hour of listening to them gripe, I left feeling depressed. If the group does not offer you support, the whole purpose for joining, or much worse, upsets you, then move on without looking back.

Remember, support groups are good for caregivers as well as those with the disease. Some days you just need an extra shoulder to lean on. As much as you love your friend or family member, there are also times that you need to share your feelings with someone else privately. This may give you the support and strength you need to provide support for others.

"Being there"

One reason people seek the support of others is as a reminder that they are not alone in times of trials and stress. If you have a friend, neighbor, or co-worker having a rough time, a quick note or phone call reminds them you care.

Something as simple as a message in e-mail can show understanding and empathy. Be there for the patient. Be there for those that are worried about the patient. You may not have all the answers – indeed, you may not have ANY of the answers, but a "Thinking about you today" card or e-mail message works wonders.

Cancer, like many things that happen to us, causes pain, confusion, fear, and sometimes, hopelessness. Even if you do not have any solutions, remember that your support is the thing

Chapter Two   Getting Support

appreciated most. Because I was worried about her, I shared my fear and concerns about Kath with my pastor and he sent me an e-mail message. I read his e-mail many times. He lost a dear friend to cancer and it reminded me that it is okay to have these feelings and that he understood.

Hi Barbara,

Sorry to hear about your friend. I myself get really ANGRY with God, the medical profession, just everything and everybody, when I see people experience so much pain and turmoil.

Yet I always come back to this: Where else and who else can I turn to but God? Sometimes the only thing we can do is pray that God be merciful.

Grace and Peace,
Pastor Don

Cancer Can't Destroy Love

Support

Come and lean on me a bit;
I know just how you feel.
I've felt your fear and loneliness;
I know your pain is real.

For I have been where you are now,
Walking that long dark road.
Then someone came to comfort me
And share my heavy load.

They helped me find new courage
And hope when I had none.
They let me lean on them awhile
'Til my battle was won.

So come and lean on me a bit,
'Til your ordeal is through.
Then find someone who needs your help,
And let them lean on you.

~ Martha J. Morrison

Chapter 3

Sometimes You Cry

Reaching Out

During that short time between diagnosis and "the news" about your condition, emotions swirl like a hurricane as you try to be optimistic, fear the worst, and deep down, dread facing whatever it will be.

On May 24, 2006, my dad had his appointment with the oncologist. When he was diagnosed, he was told "it is bad" but that day, we learned he was at stage 4. He later told me that he somehow knew that before he was told.

The hardest thing for him to do that night was to tell his daughters, so someone else did it for him. I do not remember for sure, but it may have been Karen, my stepmother.

We frequently shared our thoughts in e-mail, writing things we might not be able to say in person. I wrote the following letter to him in e-mail, not only as an encouragement, but also to let him know that I was okay, for I knew that would be one of his concerns.

Hi Daddy,

<<<<<<<< BIG HUG>>>>>>>

I've had many thoughts spinning wildly through my mind, while at the same time there's an empty void.

I know you weren't ready to talk tonight – and totally understood. I'm not sure what we'd say anyway....

I talked to Karen. When I got home, I sent a brief message to my support group. My friend Kath called but I didn't feel composed enough to talk...

but she persisted so we talked a bit. It helped me a little. She's also at stage 4.

My mind was expecting this, well to be honest, I was hoping for stage 3, but my heart wasn't ready, so it is hurting.

I called my pastor. We talked a while and it helped me. We'd talked a few days ago about the stages and what to expect. You'd like him - he has a great deal of common sense and a wonderful sense of humor. He likes to tease people... sound familiar? <G>

I told Don that I understood how it would be very hard for you to talk to us tonight. I could not imagine what I'd do if it were me, and my kids wanted to talk.

You're dealing with your own fears and stresses, and worried about Karen and your daughters. I told him that you protected us our whole lives, that we were very sheltered growing up, and you're used to being the caregiver.

I imagine that you have a great deal of things on your mind.... churning in an overwhelming current. Anger? Fear? Sorrow?

Determination? Grief? At some point, maybe hope, grace, love, and joy will be around as well.

When we were talking about you being used to being a caregiver, Don said something that was so simple, but made things seem so much easier.

He asked, "And did you and your sisters feel safe and nurtured growing up?" Yes, we most certainly did.

. "And do you all believe that Jesus Christ is your Savior?" Yes.

Then he said, "Then he has provided for his daughters and there's nothing more he need worry about. He can be at peace that you're protected from death - that in the end, there's nothing else that a parent can do more important than that."

He has a point.

Tonight, before I talked to any of my friends, I prayed. At first, there weren't any words that I could even gather, but I know that God totally understood. I pray for you that you have peace and that no matter what, you're always able to know that you aren't alone.

Chapter Three   Sometimes You Cry

It's going to be hard for everyone as you'll have good days and bad days, but let's hope that the good days are most frequent.

I know it sounds very trivial and even somewhat stupid, but I'm totally convinced that a frequent dose of laughter is important. I'm not saying it will cure anything, but it is one of the most important tools we humans have when it comes to coping.

"This is the day that the Lord has made. Let us rejoice and be glad in it." That's in Psalms, don't remember where off the top of my head. (Psalms 118:24) It's also a song.

Anyway, every day is a gift. Some gifts are better than others.... some gifts are just plain fruitcakes, the old, dried out kind that Grandma Rush used to make.

But every day you are alive, you have an opportunity to have good moments. We can all treasure these good moments, and that'll help them overshadow the bad moments.

Cancer Can't Destroy Love

I'm an optimistic person. True, I've never been diagnosed with cancer. That'd shake up even the most optimistic person.

But nevertheless, I am convinced that my optimism not only helps me cope with stressors I encounter in life, but also lessens the chances of being overwhelmed by negatives.

I know that at times when I am depressed I feel more pain and more fatigue. Even when the same things are going on, when I'm happier, it seems that there is less pain.

There will be days that you'll not only be unable to see anything except that the glass is half empty, there will be times when you'll be convinced that the glass is not even there.

Whenever you're able to remember that it's half-full, it'll be better. And some days, it will overflow.

I love you. Thank you for being the kind of dad that turned me into a responsible, patriotic, kind, faithful adult filled with a lifetime of happy memories.

Barbie

Chapter Three Sometimes You Cry

My friend Kath was diagnosed not long before my father. In both cases, when the cancer was discovered, it had already spread a great deal before there was any reason to suspect it.

Shortly after I shared Kath's condition with my pastor, he sent me a prayer to share with her. Later, when my dad received his diagnosis, I sent it to him as well.

The prayer is good, not only for the peace it brings, but because it acknowledges that sickness is not the only issue. Not only are we battling the illness, but discouragement and often, weariness.

Cancer Can't Destroy Love

A Prayer for the Sick

Lord,

You have promised us Your presence. I feel the need of that presence now for comfort, for strength. My illness saps my energy. My routine is disrupted by the unknown.

My family and friends are hurting too. Sometimes the anxiety is too much. Sometimes You seem distant. Sometimes I hurt in loneliness.

Father, heal my spirit and my body. Walk with me. Assure me that You are here. Remind me that Your grace is sufficient.

Be with those who care for me. Help me to care for them as well. Remember my fellow sufferers.

In Your grace and love, remember us all. For being here with me, thank You. Through Jesus the Christ, Amen.

Grace and Peace,

Pastor Don

Chapter Three — Sometimes You Cry

There are times when we do not know the answers to the questions we have. When life gets too overwhelming, it is hard to even remember what the questions are.

More than anything, I felt the need to reach out to my dad, to reassure him that he was not alone, that somehow, it would all work out, even though I had no idea how, and that above all, we would be okay. As a father, he had dedicated himself to doing whatever it took to provide for and protect his daughters.

His pancreatic cancer was so advanced that there was nothing that could be done. Writing through my tears, trying to be strong for him, I was struggling and needed a hug myself, but I was alone, with no hug in sight.

Just as I finished sending my message, I received a virtual hug in the form of an e-mail from my pastor, letting me know that even though he did not have the answers, he was there in spirit, holding me up. The timing was perfect. I did not need a miracle, but a reminder that someone cared, something much more valuable at that moment than all the wisdom Solomon ever possessed.

He wrote,

I'm so sorry to hear about your dad. At times like these, I wish I had the wisdom of Solomon. Maybe then, I'd have something profoundly comforting to say. As it stands, all I can do is offer you and your dad my prayers. The pain from this news must be unbearable.

Pastor Don

Chapter 4

Healing

What is healing? I was confused about that for a while. To me, if you were healed, it meant that you were made better, that your illness was gone. People told me that they were praying for healing, for my dad and for my friend. I passed the news on to my dad, hoping he would feel better about it.

A few months into the journey with cancer, we were "visiting" online around two in the morning, our usual custom, as neither could sleep well. He told me that he was just so tired and he was sorry that he was letting people down. I insisted that he was not doing that but he stated that people prayed for his complete recovery, but he let them down by staying sick.

I knew exactly what he meant. At times, I too, was uncomfortable with these prayers. When I tried to pray for healing, in my heart, I did not think that it was possible and felt so bad about it. No matter how many people told me that I should pray for healing for my dad and my friend, I just could not do it. I felt so guilty for my failure.

The next day, I spoke to my pastor about it. After sharing about our conversation, I asked, "What kind of person am I that I can not pray for my own father's healing? Why do I have so little faith?" I felt horrible and inadequate.

Then, Pastor Don asked, "What does healing mean to you?" He has an especially aggravating habit of answering my questions with more questions rather than simply telling me what I want to know. I go to him for answers, yet he most often helps me even more by having me understand and seek my own answers.

My biggest hesitation was that the only sure way I knew that they would be totally healed would be by death. As much as I wanted healing for them, I could not pray for that if it meant they would die.

When I shared that, I asked, "How could I pray for healing if the only way to get that was through death?"

He continued, "Healing is not just absence of pain or sickness. It may be coming to the point of accepting, of being at peace with the circumstances you face."

At that moment, a huge weight was lifted away. Suddenly, I completely understood, and could now pray for healing with complete acceptance and expectation that it would be done.

During our conversation, I finally understood that healing is exactly what I desired for my loved ones. Coping with the burdens placed on them by cancer would be the greatest gift I could ask for them. Acceptance and peace would be a welcome comfort.

From then on, I prayed not only for healing, but also for mercy. I thanked God for the strength that they had been given to get them through the trying times. As much as I did not want my dad to die, I wanted him to suffer even less.

I prayed for God's mercy, that they would not suffer any more than could be helped. I prayed for and expected healing, thanking God for my dad's accepting and coping, now seeking my own.

At the end, God did grant us what we asked for my dad. His battle with cancer was short and we were not ready to lose him, but he did not suffer at the end. He had a beautiful, dignified, awe-inspiring death, and God was very, very present the entire time.

He was finally, forever healed.

Chapter 5

Creating Your Perfect ATMOSPHERE

Whether you are currently dealing with cancer yourself, dealt with it in the past, are a caregiver, or just want a better, more peaceful life, then this section is for you. That would seem to cover just about everyone, right? I cannot stress this concept strongly enough. You have heard the phrase, "You are what you eat" many times. This is almost the same thing because your surroundings affect your mood, your physical well-being, and your ability to cope with life in general, if affected by cancer or not. It is important that you pay close attention to this from now on, and I will help you get started on this important life-changing quest!

What is this *atmosphere* I am referring to anyway? Well, if I were into science I would explain all about air molecules and oxygen and all sorts of highly technical terms about the stuff surrounding the earth and all around, but it's not that kind of atmosphere, so thank goodness, I won't have to do that!

This kind of atmosphere is the **environment** that you are in as well as the type of things you do with your time and efforts. In other words, the surroundings that you are in make a difference.

No, this does not mean that you can get a whole house remodel done, though if you can afford it and want that, it might not hurt! Sorry for the rest of you. Like me, you will have to deal with the current furniture.

One way to think of the type of atmosphere I am referring to is to think of your five senses, to help you concentrate on the "sensory details" of life. There is a mental component as well.

While it might take some practice at first, I can promise you, without a doubt in my mind, that once you get in the habit of maintaining this

Chapter Five	Creating Atmosphere

atmosphere, your life will be better. It will not even take extra work to achieve success!

The First Step

The first and absolutely most important step is to DECIDE that you are ready to continue. Oh sure, it sounds easy enough, but even something this simple requires a commitment. But hey, it is your life we are talking about so why not give it a shot?

Just to make it less scary, go ahead and read the rest of this so you will know what you are getting in to before deciding, but I know you will want this for yourself. Besides, you need to include all areas of your senses so learn about them all before you begin.

The easiest, but also the most important, component to master is the mental aspect because that is the one that you have the most control over. In other words, YOU can decide to a large part how you respond to things that happen.

Cancer Can't Destroy Love

You develop this skill over time. It has helped me to be aware of the "Well, it could be worse" situations in life. What if YOU are the worst-case scenario? Well, then you might want to jump to another method that works well, "Noticing the good things that are around you," without reading through to the rest of the chapter.

Noticing the Good in Life

Start small. You will not notice everything all at once. One day, maybe you see a pretty jonquil just bursting out on an early spring day. Notice it. Make a mental note in your mind, *"How nice, a pretty spring flower. Doesn't it look bright and perky?"*

Okay, you do not have to be sappy about it, but do pay close attention for those brief moments as you walk past it. Then go on. Go back to life as usual, but your mental atmosphere just shifted. You are on your way! Start sharpening your awareness of the good, pleasant, things that have been in your life all along, if you were aware of it or not.

Chapter Five   Creating Atmosphere

The next thing you know, you will notice pretty sunrises and sunsets, hear birds chirping, and smell the lilac bush blooming. You will notice the giggles of little girls playing with make-up and see squirrels scampering across the trees.

Starting to Pay Off

Not only will you begin noticing these small things, you will realize that as you do, you feel better, even if it is just for minutes at a time. No, I did not say you were cured of anything, I said you feel better! There is a difference.

When you slow down enough to notice the small things, the good things in life, then it replaces the anger and distressed thoughts in your mind for as long as you allow it to do so. You are now in control of your attitude.

You know yourself that when you are angry, your heart beats faster, you might feel sick, you breathe faster, and you do not like it. So began replacing the anger and stress with calming thoughts, good thoughts. I promise you that you will notice a positive impact on your life.

Others may soon notice a difference as well. Go ahead. It is okay to share your new "secret" for a happier, more peaceful life.

Bringing in the Sensory Details

Remember, I also told you that your five senses are involved. This is where the environmental part of the atmosphere comes into play. Think about your five senses. You know them, you learned about them in first grade, remember? There is sight, hearing, touch, taste, and smell.

That mental aspect I shared with you is also called "feelings" which some consider a part of the five senses. However, while math is not my favorite subject, I do know enough that if you add feelings, then you would have six senses so they are just "sensory wanna-bes." (Who knows? Your feelings may be quite content not being listed in the "big 5/6" and someone is just pushing a private agenda. It is possible.)

# Chapter Five	Creating Atmosphere

As you think about applying the senses to making your environment work for you, think about the things that you like. The things that work for me may not be the things that will work for you.

Do You Hear What I Hear?

Let's think about sound. If your goal is to de-stress, improve your atmosphere, and make your life better, then you need to seek out things that you enjoy. There are several things that I enjoy listening to and it depends on the mood I am in as well as my goals when I select a sound to put into my personal atmosphere.

If you are clueless and just starting out, something calming might be a good way to begin. Is that the sound of the ocean waves? Wind chimes are relaxing to me. Perhaps listening to a favorite singer helps you. Just do not trade your problems for their problems.

Choose music that will help you escape from your worries and relax, not just go from one tense situation to another. (So sorry if the songwriter's dog up and moved out and the girlfriend ran away, but you have your own issues to deal with right now.)

When I am especially upset, listening to Pachebel's "Canon in D" helps me tremendously. Handel's "Water Music" is another favorite if you enjoy classical music. Many years ago, I discovered the "Winter Solstice" CD by Wyndom Hill. They have many others out as well, but this music is at once peaceful but has enough movement to take you away from your real world.

As you consider the best sounds to immerse yourself in, do not forget silence. It may be hard to find, but at times, allowing yourself to sit quietly in a silent environment allows you to focus. As you listen to the silence or whatever sounds you choose, you may discover that you are often able to come up with insight about things you did not think possible.

Meditate. Pray. Relax.
Be yourself,
that person that you thought had disappeared.

Chapter Five   Creating Atmosphere

Starting to "Get It"

What about those other senses of taste, smell, and touch? If this requires modification to the environment, then do it if you are allowed. Some people really enjoy lighting scented candles. Others start sneezing at the mere suggestion. For many, most of the time, a little chocolate helps!

Television

Then there is television. For better or worse, this has become a staple of most households and if you have cable or similar set-ups, you can choose from hundreds of shows at once.

This can be a good thing. Television can provide an escape from reality that really helps. Get involved in the show. Enjoy it. Watch something educational and learn about new things. Learn the best way to decorate your bathroom. Laugh at a funny movie. There are many positive things that can come from watching television.

Cancer Can't Destroy Love

One of the best things about television is that you can spend a lot of time watching and lose track of time. That can be good, especially when you are sick or lonely.

One of the worst things about television is that you can spend a lot of time watching and lose track of time. Use the television as a tool, as a means of entertainment.

Ready to Begin?

Whatever you do, please do not use television as a substitute life. That is where your newfound awareness of self comes in as you work on your personal atmosphere. It is hard to focus on achieving inner peace if strangers are yelling at you from inside a box.

From personal experience, I can tell you that maintaining the right balance makes a positive difference in my life. I started paying attention to the good things around me and it made me happier.

The next thing I knew, there were more and more good things. Now it is second nature to me. I

Chapter Five   Creating Atmosphere

just naturally think on the positive side and I give partial credit to these methods I shared with you.

The most important thing to remember is to focus on the things that surround you. Purposely select things that are a help to you. Spend some quality time de-stressing and you will discover that you are recharged and ready to tackle another day, one filled with noticing more good things!

When you create a pleasant environment, or atmosphere, for your soul to breathe in, you are ultimately helping yourself lead a happier life.

No, you cannot totally shut out the bad. However, by making positive choices for the things that you can control, there is a lot less negative energy sapping your strength. You can use this energy towards coping and healing.

Balance is essential. As you learn and practice these techniques, the rest of the world continues. Spend some time listening to your favorite music. Watch some television. Listen to the quiet. Your body seeks a balance. Just quit feeding it sensory garbage.

Cancer Can't Destroy Love

Perhaps you should now get dressed in something comfortable, enjoy the smell of your brownies baking that you just know will taste great, watch the flickering light of your vanilla scented candle, and listen to your favorite music. Yes, that is a bit contrived, but only you know what works for you.

Seek what works for you.
Goal: Peace and Tranquility
Sign you made it: Coping with Life

Peace be with you.

Chapter 6

When the Dark Days Come

For years, I have lived with a chronic illness so I understand that sometimes, life gives you lemons. Some, usually those that do not seem to have problems, tell you to, "Look on the bright side" and of course, that favorite, "When life gives you lemons…" Well, you can only drink so much lemonade before you start feeling as if your body might develop a bright yellow glow as you pucker up one more time.

As you deal with cancer and everything that goes with it, your own or a loved ones', you know very well that some days you just question whether or not you can take one more step. Worse, you are not even sure you care.

Well, it may sound overly optimistic, especially if this happens to be one of those really bad days, but life gets better eventually and if you can find someone or something to help you through it, the way will be easier.

Looking on the bright side really does make a difference! I PROMISE you that! The problem on dark days, when troubles threaten to overwhelm you, is that sometimes, it is difficult to uncover that hidden bright side, and you do not have the energy or fortitude to search.

Believe me, there have been many times in my life that have been so overwhelming that it felt impossible to go on another step.

Emotional stresses as we deal with relationships, anxiety raising children, financial concerns, physical stresses due to medical conditions, and spiritual stresses all caused me to question why it was happening at times.

In my case, I do not have to handle things solo. God is here with me every step of the way. There was a time that I actually thought I was the one handling things. Silly me! Many years ago,

Chapter Six   When the Dark Days Come

there were some very serious times when we faced adversity and it seemed that there was just one thing after another going wrong no matter what we did.

Not to get bogged down in details, but twenty-five years ago, my husband and I dealt with a massive blow. We left our families and moved out of state with our six-week-old son, the only grandchild on either side, so my husband could attend Seminary. It was a leap of faith to do this, but it was only for a few short years, so what could go wrong?

Apparently, a lot of things. The quick version is that within a year of moving away from everyone we knew, my husband lost his eyesight and then his job, we had another baby, born six weeks early, and had to totally refocus our plans. You can just imagine the financial, emotional, and physical stresses we faced as one crisis after another happened that year, all away from home. As the primary caregiver, I tried to remain strong yet inside, felt as if my life were crumbling. At one point, I worried about my husband because he was so depressed that I feared he would do something drastic. My husband, as devastated as he was, dug right in, rebuilding his life, obtaining skills that would enable him to function in a new way. We were both trying to be strong for the other and for our child. If we had talked about it at the time, we might have both caved in.

When I found out that we were expecting a baby, just a week after my husband learned the devastating news about his blindness, many reacted as if that were just the final blow, more horrible news. After all, our other child was only nine months old and it was the last thing we needed.

Yet, it was not that way at all for me. Of course, it would be hard, and it was one more thing to deal with, but this baby seemed to be a message from God that life would go on, that there were good things ahead. He was my rainbow.

Certainly, the timing and the method for this particular message could have been better, but it was what I needed to be told, just as I needed it. At the time, I just tried to deal with things as they happened, trying to remain strong. Instinctively, I knew to deal with only one day at a time.

Chapter Six   When the Dark Days Come

Like cancer, the patient is not the only one affected by things like this. I did not know then what I know now, that it is important to find support, even if it is just someone to talk to privately. We both needed it.

This turned out to be a lesson for me, one that changed the way I live. While all these things were happening, we both did whatever we knew had to be done. Others marveled at our strength, but we did not have a choice. Looking back after the fact, God provided for us in ways that I had not even noticed. It just so happened that the neighborhood we moved to because it was close to the Seminary, also happened to be close to the Rehab Center my husband attended. There he started the process of getting his life back on track, and most importantly, making career connections that later changed his entire future.

Not only that, the school for visually impaired students was a mile away, even though I did not know it existed. From the age of twelve on, my goal was to teach blind children. I was already planning to be a teacher, but in college, I altered the goal at the suggestion of a misguided counselor.

How "ironic" that one of only four universities in the entire country offering the certification to teach the visually impaired, just happened to be close to where we lived and there was a scholarship for teachers going into special education that paid my entire tuition.

When we left Tennessee to move to Kentucky for three years, it certainly did not matter to us that there were so many services concerning the visually impaired within a mile of the Seminary. Yet, I am convinced that God had a hand in that as we had considered schools in two other cities, New Orleans and Dallas.

This lesson started me on my path of looking on the bright side. If things had worked out for us at such a terrible time, surely it would for more minor times. While I always believed that God was in my life before, after this experience, I knew it.

From then on, it became easier and easier for me to think positively and recognize God's

Chapter Six   When the Dark Days Come

presence. Of course, there were many rough times, but it was frequently reinforced to me that optimism made them better, though still present.

The lessons learned dealing with life changing events were messages of hope that things would work out, even though there were dark days that it did not seem possible.

One chilly, rainy winter day recently, I had a VERY bad day. As a matter of fact, it stands out in my mind as one of those "major" dark days etched in my memory. Not only was I dealing with my own serious health problems and worried about the future, I was struggling to maintain my home and faced the life changing decision to move or not.

Above all, it had only been a few months since my father had died. Christmas was survived in a state of numbness, but it got harder to cope as his birthday approached.

I cried. Not just a few tears, but I cried for hours. It was as if once the tears started, they could not be stopped. All the fears and sad thoughts that had been pushed aside came tumbling out with the tears in an uncontrollable stream. While there were occasional sobs, most of the time, the tears were just a steady flow that trickled silently down my face, like the steady rain outside. I can remember praying to God in anguished thoughts without words, as I was so distraught that words were impossible, yet I knew He understood me.

Attempts at improving my mood failed as I tried to distract myself. Even now, I recall that I wondered why I was falling apart so completely, and shared my thoughts with a friend, also named Barbara. When she heard what was going on, she said that I was just "hitting the wall" and that it was about time! After remaining as positive and upbeat as I had for so long, she thought my body and emotions had simply taken all they could handle.

The next morning, without tears but weak and feeling horrible, I read a wonderful, supportive e-mail Barbara wrote to me, sharing the words in a verse from Psalms that comforted me.

Yes, even with a positive outlook, there are dark days. Fortunately, I am blessed that they are not frequent, thanks in part to my positive attitude, which is a gift from God.

Chapter 7

The Power of Positive Thinking

Remember earlier, when I told you to notice the "good things" in life? That is an important beginning. There is research proving that those with a positive outlook have an easier time when seriously ill.

In addition, those that think positively have less stress, resulting in fewer medical complications, and it helps your body heal. Did you know that optimistic people often require lower levels of pain medications?

But forget research! I can tell you, without a shadow of doubt, that it is true. I have lived it. I know it. Surviving the dark days tested the theory.

Yet, through it all, I have been able to handle adversity without totally falling apart. No, it has not been perfect, as there have been times when I found myself on the edge. However, you can ask anyone that knows me. They often marvel that I am able to remain as calm as I have under some trying circumstances and situations.

What is my secret? It is not a secret, but more a strategy. I remain as positive as I can at all times. Being human, I slip, but then I struggle only until I remember what to do. Finally, I learned that positive thinking is the key to my survival, so I get back on track as quickly as possible in order to shake these gloomy thoughts.

About a dozen years after the onset of blindness and several children later, we were both happy in careers, had a big house, and were active in our church. Life was good. Just as it seemed that we were in a stable routine, I was diagnosed with lupus and rheumatoid arthritis. This has had difficulties, but one doctor almost messed me up. He was rather gloomy in his prognosis and warned

Chapter Seven   The Power of Positive Thinking

me that it would probably kill me within at most, seven to ten years.

You can imagine how devastating that was, especially since we had a houseful of kids between the ages of one and thirteen that I feared I would not live to raise. Well, God was my rock before and became a boulder then. One tearful night, I turned it ALL over to Him and from then on, knew it would all work out for the best. Since then, I can honestly say that although there have been more serious things to worry about, I rarely feel upset. There is a calmness and peace because I know that God is handling it all for me.

The first thing I did was to get a different doctor because I instinctively knew that his attitude was not what I needed. Even though there have been some very rough times since then as lupus progressed, now, almost fifteen years later, I am still here and do not plan on leaving any time soon. Who knows what happened to that gloomy doctor that was so wrong in his prediction?

That fifteen-year period changed my whole outlook. I grew stronger and stronger in my faith, constantly seeing the good in the things around me, even as very bad things continued to happen, but I did not do it alone.

Lupus kept up an attack and though my health continuously deteriorated, it has been possible to see the good in things, and to feel at peace. God is my strength and gives me a positive attitude. Without doubt, this is not something I could have done on my own. My support group is there to cheer when life goes well and provides a shoulder when needed, but God provides the peace.

Just as we were in the "right place at the right time" so many years earlier, there just "happen" to be the right people in the right place for me now. They are here for me, even if all I need is to know that they are available and that they care.

In addition to your personal happiness and well being, having a positive attitude affects those around you. I know of a woman that never seems to think positively. Even if you just say hello to her, she looks at the negative. I try to turn her around and mention how nice the weather is but she says, "It will get colder next week." Heaven forbid

Chapter Seven   The Power of Positive Thinking

someone asks, "How are you today?" in that polite way of socializing because it leads to a whole list of physical complaints.

Not only do you feel better when you have a positive outlook, others will want you around. Obviously, the grouchy woman I told you about spends a lot of time alone, which may reinforce her negative thoughts.

Positive thinking is closely related to the practice of optimism as you begin looking at the bright side of things, but it is actually more complex. Looking at life in this way involves trust and an *expectation* that things will be okay. Unfortunately, I cannot tell you that expecting things to be okay will result in less heartache and that you will be cured of cancer or anything else. It is partially just accepting reality with a peaceful heart, with a calmness and reassurance that no matter what the future holds, you will be able to cope. My life is proof.

However, that does not mean that you can give up hope. Even if the point comes when death is inevitable, there is still reason to be joyful knowing pain and suffering will end, though sadness for the family seems unbearable at the time.

One thing that works for me is to surround myself with positive images and pictures of peaceful places. When I walk in my front door every afternoon, one of the first things I see is a sign that reminds me to, *"Make time for the quiet moments as God whispers and the world is loud."* Looking in one direction, the words *"Believe"* and in another, *"Inspire"* are located in the rooms.

My goal in life is not to live forever, or even to live to become elderly. That is not realistic and I would be setting myself up for disappointment. No, for quite a while, my goal has been to handle whatever comes my way with as much grace and good will as I can muster, making a positive difference to those around me as much as possible.

Every morning, as I get ready, I see Reinhold Niebuhr's well-known "Serenity Poem" on my bathroom wall. It helps keep me focused as I remember my goals.

Chapter Seven   The Power of Positive Thinking

Serenity
"God grant me the serenity to
ACCEPT the things I cannot change;
COURAGE to change the things I can;
and the WISDOM to know the difference."

There is more to his poem.

Living one day at a time,
enjoying one moment at a time,
accepting hardship
as a pathway to peace,
taking this sinful world as it is,
not as I would have it;

trusting that you will make
all things right
if I surrender to Your Will;
so that I may be reasonably happy
in this life and
supremely happy
with you forever in the next.

Cancer Can't Destroy Love

Cancer and other illnesses can destroy your body, but not your spirit, unless you allow it to do so. Whether it is cancer, chronic illness, or other conditions trying to take away your peace, live each day as fully as possible, not worrying about the next day. For as much or as little as you can do, then that is your goal for the day. Do not beat yourself up over what cannot be done, but celebrate and rejoice in what is possible.

Chapter 8

Profiles in Courage

Cancer steals more than the physical aspects of our lives. It touches the emotional, spiritual, and relational as well. At times, there seems to be little that we can do, as the disease devours the body, devastating us. Yet, despite cancer's attempts to break down the system, it does not always win.

Sometimes, cancer loses when the patient is healed and cancer is cast out. What a victory! Other times, the disease remains, but the human spirit overcomes, so that it would be impossible to say that cancer actually won.

Despite a grim prognosis, my father was able to make peace within his heart, robbing cancer of a true victory. He frequently said, "I never thought I would get cancer. I always figured it would be my heart." Both of his parents died of heart disease and we too, expected that he would one day have a heart attack. However, it was cancer that took him from us, though he left a legacy of doing the right thing and serving others that lives on after his death.

My friend Kath, whom you have "met" throughout this book, has been an inspiration to me, long before cancer entered the picture. When we met, she was a single mother struggling with raising her girls on her own, and dealing with life-threatening issues as the result of lupus. She needed a wheelchair to get around. At one point, she had to have breathing treatments several times a day.

Despite what was at times, a bleak existence, she persevered and kept a very positive attitude, always quick to support others. She fought back bravely and her hard work and determination has been an inspiration for countless people.

Eventually, after much therapy and hard work, she was able to walk again; something most felt was impossible. While others would have given up long ago, she kept going. With great joy, we celebrated as she gained new loves in her life, her new husband, Andre', and then her two precious grandsons and a granddaughter.

Then, after several months of extensive bleeding, Andre' rushed her to the hospital emergency room knowing it simply was not normal, despite what her doctors said. That is when we heard the devastating, unexpected news. It was cancer and her prognosis was grim.

However, a year later, she led a team in *The Underwear Affair*, an event in Canada similar to the Relay for Life in the United States. It is a 5km walk or a 10 km run that brings awareness to cancers that take place below the waist. Their team, called the "Knaughty Knickers," raised over $11,000.00.

Years before, she could not walk at all, yet despite suffering with serious issues due to lupus, and then actively and aggressively treating cancer, she walked triumphantly!

The facts? She has two kinds of uterine cancer, one Endometrial, and the other Uterine Papillary Serous Carcinoma Stage IV with metastasis to the lymph nodes. After extensive and invasive surgery, she was left with macroscopic disease that could not be removed because of the location attached to a vein in her groin. Kath had six chemotherapy treatments of Taxol and Carboplatin followed by seven weeks of Radiation therapy and Brachytherapy.

She still suffers from side effects of both treatments with peripheral neuropathy, and never ending diarrhea. As expected, the disease and treatments made her existing Lupus flare up. Every three months, they check for any recurrences requiring further treatment. The recurrence rate is high and prognosis dismal for this cancer, so we are all blessed that she has have come so far!

Kath has been aware of this book and encouraged me to write it, never suspecting until the end that she was a part of it. I gave her an opportunity to share a message about cancer.

Chapter Eight   Profiles in Courage

Two Things I Would Like to Share with the World

By Katherine Kilcullen-Bergeron

To let other young women know that maybe if I had been a bit more aggressive with the doctors my outcome would have been different. When I presented myself with constant bleeding at age 46, I was told that it was 'normal' peri-menopausal symptoms. I later discovered that was not true, that the bleeding should have been investigated and my cancer prognosis is not good because of it.

Although I am doing well thus far, it is always on my mind that maybe I could have done more to help myself earlier on, and my family would not have to suffer so much now. Maybe we can save a life if someone gets the proper treatment earlier?

I can endure the pain and treatments because I am not alone. I have a loving family and dear friends looking out for me every step I take. I have never traveled this path alone. I think that is what Faith really is, knowing that you are never really alone, whether it is your loved ones by your side, or in your darkest hours when you know that God is there with you too.

I do what I need medically, holistically, and spiritually to help myself, but in the end, it is the love of my family and friends that gives me the strength to continue to fight the good fight. They are the most important part of my medical team, and treatment plan. Their love carries me through. I am hopeful that I will recover and beat the cancer, but if I don't I am not scared of dying. I know the adults in my life know that I never give up. My only fear is that my grandson Isaac will be totally crushed, and my prayer is that I survive this cancer so that he never need to know that pain, and if that fails, I pray that Isaac finds huge strength in his little heart to know that he will always be in mine, even if he can't see me. I would never leave him by choice, and should I die, he is to know that I would then always be his very own special angel.

The news of a family member having cancer is a crushing blow to any family. When a loved one

Chapter Eight   Profiles in Courage

dies, then that blow becomes final. Your dad fought the good fight, and he was surrounded by such loving family. I am blessed that I consider you part of my family too.

Love,
Kath

Kath is a role model and an inspiration to all that know and love her. She serves as a reminder that despite what "should" be, it is sometimes possible to beat the odds, or at least put things off. The cancer treatments made the lupus worse. The lupus treatments made the cancer worse. In the end, there is little that can be done for her. Kath's faith in God, emotional strength, and determination have given her time, precious time she spends making the world better for others.

Cancer Can't Destroy Love

These two people, my father and my friend, are just symbols of the many others affected by cancer. Like them, there are so many with similar stories.

If cancer has affected you, a loved one, or both, you know the courage they have shown. Keep the faith and do not give up. Cancer may seem to take everything, but it cannot truly win, as long as you do not allow it to do so.

Chapter 9

After Cancer

If this chapter pertains to you, or if you are just reading it so you will be prepared, you know that your life has changed in many ways.

For one thing, you learned that the only way to get through the treatment was to deal only with those things you had to deal with. Normal life, whatever that is, was put on hold as the entire family's focus was on cancer for the time period.

In the meantime, you were "out of the loop" and it may or may not be easy to jump back in. Perhaps you are not even sure that you want back in. My friend Alex, another member of our support group, has learned this all too well as her husband Jesse has dealt with cancer, remissions, and recurrences most of the time we have known each other. She shared how hard it was to see friends disappear, because you did not have the time available to spend nurturing that friendship, or because they did not feel comfortable.

Coping with cancer is more than a physical, psychological, or mental battle. It is stressful to deal with all that is going on. Medical appointments dominate your schedule as you go for doctor appointments, tests, and treatments.

Alex shared that one of the things that is hard is when you must stop attending community events such as church or ballgames. Part of it is being too tired or sick, but the patient often must avoid large groups of people because of weakened immune systems.

As you prioritized the things that were important to you, perhaps for the first time, it may be that some of the things that used to take up all your time are no longer of interest.

In addition to changes in activities, you may have seen changes in the people around you. There are new people that you met during this time that are special as well as former friends.

Chapter Nine — After Cancer

Unfortunately, some friends were scarce during this time. Chronic conditions and long-term issues confuse some people. They expect things to be "over" quickly so things get back to normal. When it does not, they do not have a back-up plan.

Many people are uncomfortable around cancer or around long-term sicknesses in general. They remind me of basketball fans that are the teams' biggest supporters as long as they have a winning season but are the first to complain and drop off as the team struggles.

Other friends were there with you throughout. They took you to chemo treatments, sat up with you, sent encouraging cards, mowed your grass without being asked, and fed your dog when you were unable to do so. That is the difference between a friend that nurtures you, and one that is "just a friend."

Not only have friendships changed, it is quite possible that you have changed as well. As you grew emotionally, and perhaps, spiritually, your attitudes may have shifted. In this case, past friendships may not be as much a part of your life.

Good or bad, facts are facts. Hopefully, you have not been hurt and suffered the loss of a friendship or loved one.

Now, after cancer, it is time to live the rest of your life. Your diet, self-esteem, and lifestyle may have changed. Whether you were the patient or a loved one, after cancer touched your life, you are not quite the same person. Whatever the effect, move on, as you gain new perspectives and strength along the way. Life continues. You can make it!

Chapter 10

Fighting Back: The Relay for Life

One of the biggest fundraisers for the American Cancer Society is the Relay for Life. It is also one of their most well known activities.

The Relay for Life celebrates those that survive, hoping to increase that number. Funds raised go towards research and to support cancer patients as they battle the disease. Not all those diagnosed with cancer become Survivors. That is the purpose of raising funds for cancer research, so we can change that fact.

For those that are not familiar with the Relay, it is a community-wide event. Some groups raise money all year while others start shortly before the event. Individuals, schools, businesses, and church groups get involved to raise money turned in at the Relay.

Many colleges host a Relay for Life and the teams are made of various school clubs and organizations, many of whom compete with each other to raise the most money.

Sometimes families and groups form a team in honor or in memory of a loved one with cancer. Other times, teams are more general, but members are very likely to have some type of experience with cancer. It may be personally, through a friend, or perhaps, a loved one.

In addition to raising money all along, the teams attend the Relay for Life, usually held at a large location such as a school. Each team has a booth or some other space to gather. Some teams raise money with activities at their booth. They may offer games, foods, or other treats.

During the night, members of the teams walk around the track. It is not usually too strenuous and along the way, you can visit with friends. There is a goal to try to have at least one member of your team walking at all times. One way of raising

Chapter Ten   Fighting Back: The Relay for Life

money is to have people pledge a certain amount based on the number of laps walked around the track, though most people donate a set amount.

There are contests, fun activities, and plenty of food to eat. Many times, there are live bands for your listening pleasure. The teams often decorate their booths and some may even dress alike.

Our church is fairly small when compared to others in our local area, but you cannot tell it by our impact in the community. Members frequently reach out to others and volunteer freely in many activities such as mission trips, cleaning up the community, a nursing home ministry, working with the homeless, helping those with unique needs, and other activities. We do not hesitate to help.

It is no surprise that this little stone church on the corner in a small town stepped up to form a team, one of the few church groups at the Relay last year. Our Praise Team sang, we had carnival games for kids, and we sold hot dogs. We may only have 125 members on Sunday mornings, yet we raised over $2,700.00! Church groups donated money and we collected items for our basket sold at the Silent

Auction. Our "No-Bake Bake Sale" was a very successful fund-raiser.

In every group of people, you will find those that have been touched by cancer in some way, and church is no exception. We put up lavender and purple stars around the doors of the sanctuary. Each star was "in honor of" someone that had survived cancer or "in memory of" those that had not. There were so many stars! It was for them that we joined the Relay in order to put an end to cancer.

Chapter 11

Reflections on the Night

The Relay for Life serves as a gathering place for those in the community that have a mutual story to tell, a night of shared hopes. Some are celebrating another year away from cancer, while others may be facing it again, or with someone else. People may be there in memory of friends and family members that could not be there. All are present with the purpose of preventing others from suffering the pain that they endured.

While the evening is about having fun and raising money for research, there are two unique moments that are especially touching and significant, the Survivors Lap and the Luminaria.

The Survivors Lap:
A Celebration

While the Relay for Life raises money for cancer research, it is promoted as a celebration, or in honor of, those that made it, "The Survivors."

After the opening ceremonies, the first lap around the track is, "The Survivors Lap." They may have just recently survived the battle or might be celebrating total recovery and years of cancer-free living. While other laps are walked by all, only the Survivors participate in the first one.

It would stand to reason that someone as emotional as I am would have difficulty with this Relay for Life celebration of those that survived. Just as I cry when I think about the birth of a baby, I cry when I think of those that survive cancer. It was a joyous moment.

Last year, as I watched my friends, B.J. and Vicki, walk hand in hand, full of smiles, it was very touching to me. They both survived cancer. They survived not only having the disease themselves, but survived as the caregiver of the other.

Chapter Eleven   Reflections on the Night

They live with the realization that sometimes, cancer comes back. They smiled going around the track. They had survived. BJ still gets tired easily and has to drink water frequently now, because of surgery for his disease, but they had still survived, serving as an encouragement for others.

I watched the crowd around me as the Survivors walked around. Many of those watching had been the caregivers. Their expressions showed pride, with a hint of memories, and their relief.

While they smiled, many, like me, also cried. They remembered the day they heard the diagnosis, the days of treatments, the discouragement, and the many hours sitting up worried and praying, the good days and bad, days spent supporting the smiling person that walked around the track.

That made the celebration of the Survivors Lap that much more special.

Cancer Can't Destroy Love

The Luminaria

As I watched the Survivors and the loved ones on the sidelines, like others there with me, it was a bittersweet evening. Thoughts of survivors, but also memories of those that lost the battle, filled my head.

Unfortunately, for all that survive, there are those that did not. I thought of my aunt, of teachers, of friends. I thought of my feisty friend Bev. We all said, "If anyone could beat cancer, it'd be Bev," but we were wrong. Perhaps they won a few battles for a while, but then, when cancer returned, they lost the cruel war.

Or maybe they were like my father. Six months after going in for what we thought was a routine gall bladder surgery, we buried him. In the process of preparing for surgery, they discovered that he had pancreatic cancer. He lost his only battle with cancer, one that was far too short.

Cancer does not fight fair. The path is rocky and the disease can lurk silently, destroying healthy cells long before we are even aware that it exists.

Chapter Eleven — Reflections on the Night

At the Relay for Life last year, as I watched the Survivors take their lap, I also thought of my dad. The spring before, just a year earlier, he thought his life was on track and it was smooth sailing ahead. By the fall, he lost his only battle with pancreatic cancer.

While the teams usually spend the night and there are activities to do, one of the most special events, held near the end of the evening, is called the "Luminaria."

For this event, they put out sand filled bags with a candle in it around the track. My family bought bags in honor of teachers, and in memory of Bev and my dad. Each bag, either "In Honor" of someone living with cancer or a Survivor, or "In Memory" of someone that did not make it, shines out like a beacon of hope for the future.

The bags are arranged in an endless circle, but they are no longer bags of sand with a candle inside. As they are lighted and shine in the dark spring night, they are transformed in some beautiful, magical way.

Cancer Can't Destroy Love

Muted lights flicker bravely, creating a shimmering beauty that is unmatched by any other. It is breathtaking, at once calming and uplifting. It is a reminder of the many people touched by cancer. For every one of the softly glowing lights, there were dozens of people affected.

Walking around the track, you see the names, some that you recognize, of those that are special to someone there. Each name, while highlighting a loved one, was yet another way of raising funds in the fight against this disease.

When you see the name of your own loved one, it is a touching moment. It was as if he were with me in some way.

I had a hard time viewing the Luminaria last year. I felt more alone than I recall being in my entire life. Although I was there with a group, none were with me at that moment.

While I was alone in body, my soul was not alone. I felt God's embrace holding me up, and held tight many loving memories of my father. As hard as it was without him, I knew I would survive, for I was not truly alone.

Chapter Eleven Reflections on the Night

Perhaps that is appropriate. While the person with cancer seems most affected, the loved ones are scarred for life as well. Even if surrounded by friends and other family members, each person makes his or her own peace, or not, with cancer individually. Sometimes, it takes time. Sometimes, it never happens.

As I prayed for the people still fighting, and celebrated with those that had survived, I also remember saying over and over to myself, "It's not fair. It's not fair."

One of the things that my father frequently told my sisters and me growing up, and later, his grandchildren, is that "Life is not fair. Deal with it." He lived that in the way that he dealt with cancer, never losing his dignity or sense of responsibility towards his family.

My father was a good man, well loved by so many. He was kind and never knew a stranger.

No, it is not fair. Cancer is never fair.

Cancer Can't Destroy Love

What Cancer Cannot Do

Cancer is so limited...

It cannot cripple love,

It cannot shatter hope,

It cannot corrode faith,

It cannot destroy peace,

It cannot kill friendship,

It cannot suppress memories,

It cannot silence courage,

It cannot invade the soul,

It cannot steal eternal life,

It cannot conquer the spirit.

.

Cancer is so limited.

~ Author Unknown

Chapter 12

Resources

The following pages give a list of organizations that specialize in Cancer Education, Treatment, and Hospice Care. While not a complete listing, you should be able to locate resources for your area. Website information is given when available. These websites often provide other links of interest to you.

Cancer Can't Destroy Love

Canadian Resources

CANCER INFORMATION

Canadian Cancer Society
http://www.cancer.ca

    National Office
    Suite 200, 10 Alcorn Avenue
    Toronto, Ontario M4V 3B1
    1-888-939-3333

Canadian Health Network
    e-mail: chn-info-rcs@phac-aspc.gc.ca

    Public Health Agency of Canada
    10th Floor, Jeanne Mance Building
    Tunney's Pasture, A.L. 1910B
    Ottawa, Ontario
    K1A 0K9

HOSPICE and COPING SERVICES

Alberta Hospice Palliative Care Association
    e-mail: pcareab@telus.net

    c/o Pilgrims Hospice Society
    9808 148 Street
    Edmonton, AB T5N 3E8
    (780) 454-4848

Chapter Twelve   Resources - Canada

British Columbia Palliative Care Association
http://www.hospicebc.org
e-mail: bchpca@cheos.ubc.ca

   Room 502, Comox Building
   1081 Burrard Street
   Vancouver, BC V6Z 1Y6
   (604) 806-8821
   toll-free: 1-877-422-4722
   fax: 604-806-8822

Canadian/Provincial Hospice Organizations
http://www.chpca.net

   Canadian Hospice/Palliative Care Association
   Annex B, Saint-Vincent Hospital
   60 Cambridge St. North, Ottawa,
   ON K1R 7A5
   (613) 241-3663
   toll-free: 1-800-286-9755
   fax: (613) 241-3986

Hospice & Palliative Care Manitoba
http://www.manitobahospice.mb.ca
e-mail: info@manitobahospice.mb.ca

   2109 Portage Avenue
   Winnipeg, MB R3J 0L3
   (204) 889-8525
   toll-free: 1-800-539-0295
   fax: 204-888-8874

Hospice Association of Ontario
http://www.hopsice.on.ca
e-mail: info@hospice.on.ca

2 Carlton Street, Suite 707
Toronto, ON M5B 1J3
toll-free: 1-800-349-3111
fax: 416-304-1479

Hospice Palliative Care Association of Prince Edward Island
http://www.hospicepei.ca
e-mail: hpca@hospicepei.ca

5 Brighton Road
Charlottetown, PE C1A 8T6
(902) 368-4498   fax: 902-368-4095

New Brunswick Hospice Palliative Care Association
e-mail: psomerville@nb.aibn.com

c/o 280 Connaught Street, Apartment 24
Fredericton, NB E3B 2B4
(506) 452-9310

Newfoundland & Labrador Palliative Care Association
http://www.nlpca.info
e-mail: laurieanne.obrien@hccsj.nl.ca

100 Forrest Road
St. John's, NF A1A 1E5
(709) 777-8638

Chapter Twelve   Resources - Canada

Nova Scotia Hospice Palliative Care Association
http://www.nshpca.ca
e-mail: amckim@chdha.nshealth.ca

    c/o Colchester Regional Hospital
    Truro, NS B2H 5A1
    (902)   893-7171   fax: 902-893-7172

Ontario Palliative Care Association
    e-mail: opca@neptune.on.ca

    194 Eagle Street
    Newmarket, ON L3Y 1J6
    (905) 954-0938
    toll-free: 1-888-379-6666
    fax: 905-954-0939

Réseau de soins palliatifs du Québec
http://www.reseaupalliatif.org
e-mail: info@aqsp.org

    500 rue Sherbrooke Ouest, bureau 900
    Montréal, QC H3A 3C6
    (514) 282-3808   fax: 514-844-7556

Saskatchewan Hospice Palliative Care Association
http://saskpalliativecare.com
e-mail: saskpalliativecare@saqsktel.net

    Box 37053
    Regina, SK S4S 7K3
    (306) 585-2871   fax: (306) 790-8634

OTHER RESOURCES

Childhood Cancer Foundation
   http://www.candlelighters.ca/
   http://www.childhoodcancer.ca
   e-mail: info@childhoodcancer.ca

   Childhood Cancer Foundation
   Candlelighters Canada
   1300 Yonge Street, Suite #405
   Toronto, Ontario M4T 1X3
   (416) 489-6440
   toll-free 1-800-363-1062
   fax: (416) 489-9812

This organization was established to support children and families dealing with childhood cancer. The website provides informational links, information about cancer, support groups, and activities for participation in fundraising to wipe out cancer.

Underwear Affair, Segal Cancer Centre
   http://www.uncoverthecure.org/index.html
   e-mail: infomontreal@uncoverthecure.org

   Phone 514-287-CURE (514-287-2873)

"Uncover the Cure." This is the 10K run and 5K walk that Kath participated in. There are links for the various places on the website. They promote an awareness and funding for cancers below the waist.

Chapter Twelve   Resources –United States

US Resources

CANCER INFORMATION

American Cancer Society
http://www.cancer.org/docroot/home/index.asp

1-800-ACS-2345 (1-800-227-2345)

The website gives extensive information on all types of cancer, research, links to local resources, a forum and blog. They also link to the Relay for Life and other activities.

National Cancer Institute
http://www.cancer.gov
http://cis.nci.nih.gov/resources/resources.html

NCI Public Inquiries Office
6116 Executive Boulevard, Room 3036A
Bethesda, MD 20892-8322
1-800-4 CANCER (1-800-422-6237)

Information about cancer from screenings to treatments. The website shares information about many types of cancer. They also list information about cancer research, drugs commonly used, and trials as well as other resources for families. Link to the "Cancer Survivors Network." There are more than 3,400 offices nationwide.

Cancer Can't Destroy Love

HOSPICE and COPING SERVICES

Hosparus; The Community Hospices of Louisville,
  Southern Indiana, and Central Kentucky
  http://www.hosparus.org
  Toll free (800) 264-0521

Hosparus is a non-profit organization that helps patients and families face life-limiting and end of life care in a peaceful and dignified way. The patient care number is available 24/7. Bereavement services are also offered. The website has extensive links and information.

Hospice Foundation of America
  http://www.hospicefoundation.org/

Their mission is to help patients and caregivers deal with terminal illnesses, death, and grief. Website links give nationwide information.

Chapter Twelve   Resources –United States

National Hospice & Palliative Care Organization
(NHPCO)
http://www.caringinfo.org
e-mail: nhpcp_info!nhpco.org

1700 Diagonal Road, Suite 625
Alexandria, Virginia 22314
(703) 837-1500
fax: 703/837-1233
HelpLine (800) 658-8898

The National Hospice and Palliative Care Organization and the National Hospice Foundation have created a consumer-focused group called Caring Connections. The Help Line gives consumer information.

OncoLink
http://www.oncolink.com/coping/
Operated by the Abramson Cancer Center of the University of Pennsylvania

This is an online resource for helping patients as well as caregivers cope with cancer. Information is available about cancer, hospice, diet, and supporting one another.

OTHER RESOURCES

Make-A-Wish Foundation® of America
http://www.wish.org/

    3550 North Central Avenue, Suite 300
    Phoenix, Arizona 85012-2127
    (602) 279-WISH (9474)
    toll-free: (800) 722-WISH (9474)
    fax: (602) 279-0855

This organization helps make wishes come true for children diagnosed with life threatening medical conditions.

Relay for Life (American Cancer Society)
    http://www.relayforlife.org/relay/

To speak to someone about the Relay, please contact the American Cancer Society, listed above. At the website, you can use a map to locate events near you, learn how to form and join teams, get fundraising ideas, and other resources. The website has informational links as well as online forums for users information.

Personal Resources

Author's Note

When we began this journey together, I told you that you would learn how to defeat cancer. Hopefully, you now have the encouragement and tools you need to battle this foe. The e-mail messages included have not been edited or screened in any way. When they were written, it was not with any thoughts of inclusion in a book, but they were just personal messages written in support. They are included, with permission, because they are a part of the story, ribbons that are intertwined in this event we call life.

Each person has a slightly different journey, and as a unique individual, brings different skills, experiences, and concerns along as baggage. Therefore, the solution is unique as well. All I can do is to offer you encouragement and share my strategies for survival. You can model your own strategies after these or use the inspiration to discover those that work best for you. While a unique route at times, the journey may be the same.

The chapters about the Relay for Life were written first, at a time when my emotions were raw and I was hurting emotionally as well as physically. The rest of the book was written almost a year later because I knew how hard it had been for me to survive even with the strategies I had discovered along my own journey. If I can help ease the way of others, then this book has served its purpose.

Now, almost two years since my father was taken from me by cancer, I have begun a healing process, but it will never end as long as I remember him. But that is as it should be. It is in his honor that

I share this book with others now, knowing he would wholeheartedly support it. It would satisfy and comfort him to know that the lessons he taught us as he fought cancer were not in vain.

Cancer takes without permission, but we can fight with everything we have, including our thoughts. If I could wave a magic wand and make your way easier, I would, but unfortunately, we all must live each day out, one by one. Now you have some strategies to give you a fighting chance. Some days are just plain rotten and we simply have to get through them, but whenever it is possible, try to have a good day!

Credits

My friend Vicki, a cancer survivor that lost both her parents to cancer, shared the moving poem, "What Cancer Cannot Do" with me when I lost my father. I have since seen it many other times and places, but have been unable to track down the author.

The poem, "Support," by Martha J. Morrison, was used with permission and encouragement by the Oldham County (Kentucky) Breast Cancer Support Team. Contact Linda Glover (502) 222-3304, ext. 3618 for more information.

The photos on the cover are courtesy of Richard Weisser and SmokyPhotos.com. They were taken around the Great Smoky Mountains National Park, one of my dad's favorite places to fish.

www.ingramcontent.com/pod-product-compliance
Lightning Source LLC
Chambersburg PA
CBHW051707040426
42446CB00008B/752